How to Draw Krappy Kartoons really well

Geoff Kelly

ALLEN&UNWIN

First published 2006

Copyright © text and illustrations, Geoff Kelly 2006

Allen & Unwin
83 Alexander St
Crows Nest NSW 2065
Australia
Phone: (61 2) 8425 0100
Fax: (61 2) 9906 2218
Email: info@allenandunwin.com
Web: www.allenandunwin.com

National Library of Australia
Cataloguing-in-Publication entry:

Kelly, Geoff.
How to draw krappy kartoons really well.

For children.
ISBN 1 74114 760 3.

1. Cartooning - Technique - Juvenile literature. I. Title.

741.5

Designed by Sandra Nobes
Set in Cafeteria by Tou-Can Design
Printed by McPhersons Printing Group, Australia

1 3 5 7 9 10 8 6 4 2

Contents

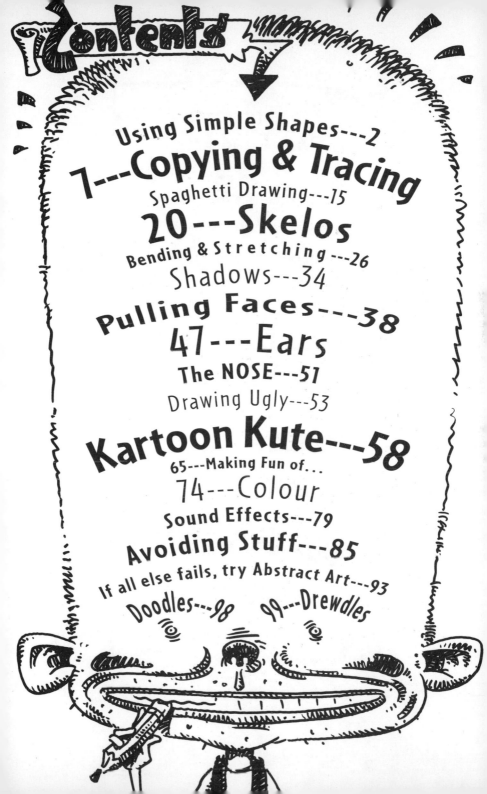

Foreword from a
Famous Dead Artist

Dear Krappy Kartoonist,

Don't make the same mistake I did and wait until you're decomposing before you become RICH & FAMOUS!
— It Stinks!!! —
Start now! All you need to know is in this book.

If you are reading this book it means you're smart enough to know that you are a **KRAPPY DRAWER!!!** Good! It also means that you are holding the book the right way up and that you have at least one eyeball!

VERY GOOD!!! Yep, all clear signs that you have what it takes to **succeed** in the **world of Art**. So read on...

Ready? Let's go...

Using Simple Shapes!

OK, everyone has seen those
'How to Draw' books that use simple shapes as a base
for drawing all sorts of cool things.

EXAMPLE A Cartoon Starfish

① Start with simple shape

② Round off and add detail

③ Add features

WOW, it looks **SO EASY!** But the big question is – when
it's not a starfish, how do you know **WHICH** shapes to
start off with in the first place? The answer is **research!**
You have to get to know your subject **INSIDE OUT!**
So, here's the bit the other books never bothered to tell you.

2

Suppose you want to draw a cute little kitten like this.
How do you work out which shapes you'll need?

The first thing to do is to simplify the outlines.
So let's start by **SHAVING OUR KITTEN!**

Now strip off the skin and those shapes will **really** start to reveal themselves!

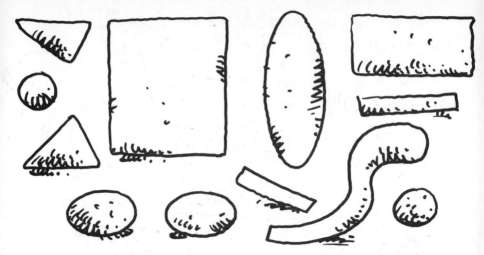

Hmm...OK. Pick up all the shapes and arrange neatly.
We now have everything we need to draw
our cute little kitten.

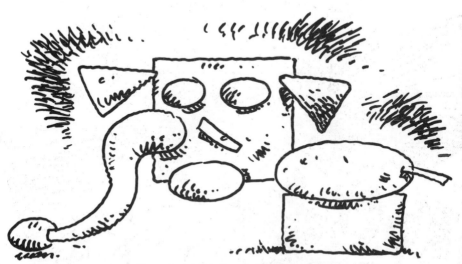

Er...I think that's how it goes?
Let's put the skin back on and see...

GULP! I think this kitten **BADLY** needs some **FUR!!!**

So there you have it – a cute woolly mammoth. **MAMMOTH!!!**
Hmm…OK, look, I think it would be best for everyone
if we just moved on to the next chapter! Don't you???

Copying & Tracing

Don't let anyone tell you that copying and tracing are **wrong**. They are two of the most important skills for fast-tracking successful **Krappy Kartoons.**

But hold on- aren't they, like, CHEATING?!!!

Well, to some people they are! But really, SO WHAT? Look, when kids start MUSIC, they are encouraged to learn and practise songs written by other people! But in ART, it's – 'No way, pal, here are some crayons and a blank sheet of paper...CREATE A MASTERPIECE!' In music it'd be like giving someone a recorder for the first time and expecting them to write a 'Top 40' Hit!

You are _so_ right !!! So how does it work?

OK, it's like this.

I can see my house from up here.

Me on my High Horse

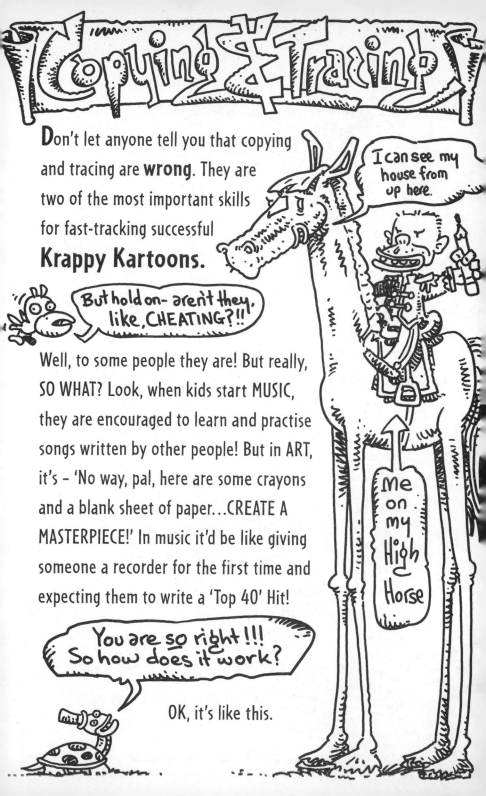

Let's use dancing as an example. The best and quickest way to **learn to dance** is to practise with an experienced partner, right? Well, drawing is the same. When you are tracing a picture you are really drawing/dancing with the artist! **COOL, HEY?!!**

And the more you trace the better you'll get, because you're learning from a pro! And once you've learnt all the steps you can then go off and dance to your own beat.

DID YOU KNOW?

The first ever **ARTWORK** was actually a **TRACING!!!** 'How can that be?', I hear you say. 'How can you **TRACE** something that doesn't yet exist?' A bit like the chicken or the egg. OK, the best way to explain this astounding **FACT** is to tell a little story - the **story** of...

TAG the Caveman

Tag lived a long time ago,
before just about anything had really happened!

His favourite thing to eat were
the wild berries growing on the
bushes in his valley.

One day it began to rain.
With umbrellas not yet
invented, Tag got soaked
running back to his cave.

Towels also were in short supply...
Tag began to shiver as he sat eating his soggy berries.

9

Poor Tag.
He suddenly felt a **sneeze** coming on!!!

"Sniff" "Sniff"

Ahh...

Ahhh...

AAhhh...

Choooo...

As he put his hand out to steady himself against the wall,
Tag let go an almighty STICKY BERRY SNEEZE!

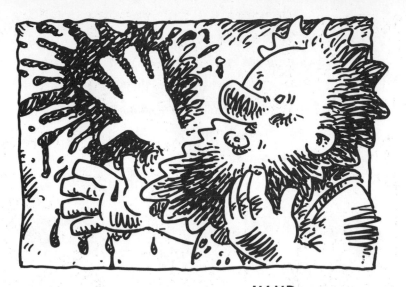

When Tag looked up he discovered a HAND just like his PAINTED on the WALL! The first ever 'Work of Art'! (And what's more, it was a tracing.)

His cold lasted about a week, and by that time he had a whole wall of hands to show off. The exhibition was a **great success!** Cave folk came from all over to marvel at Tag's remarkable new invention.

They soon started to ask him to decorate their drab, ordinary caves. Tag (whose name is still identified with painting walls) moved on from **HANDS** to **FEET** and then for a short time, **HEADS**. But as nobody likes having someone sneeze into their face, especially with a mouthful of berries, he eventually began specialising in large furry mammals **– which became very popular!**

So, all art since can **TRACE** its roots back to **Tag** and his **original big sneeze**.

Now that ART has been invented, we can talk about COPYING.
Everyone copies. **EVERYONE!** And it's a very good thing
that they do because it's the basic reason we have
a culture and aren't still all painting with berries.

Look at Ancient Egypt with all those four-sided pyramids.

Now don't tell me they didn't know about the
CONE  or the CUBE or even the
DODECAHEDRON.
Of course they did, but they were too busy copying
each other to **try anything new.**

Which is kind of handy as it makes it easy now for us
to recognise **Egyptian Art**. Because of all that copying,
everything looks so much **alike**.

13

ALIKE, yes, but always **SLIGHTLY** different. Copies are never quite the same, which is how Art changes and slowly becomes new. So next time you get caught copying (as long as it's not in a maths test) just say that you're busy, advancing AUSTRALIAN CULTURE!

Oh, and the reason Egyptians always drew people with eyes on the sides of their heads is that they were always watching what everyone else was doing!

DID YOU KNOW?

Ancient Egypt was the first and greatest of the Krappy Kartoon civilisations. Look at what they invented!

Speech bubbles

Funny faces on things

Silly hats

Strange little characters

Animal heads on human bodies

Cartoon strips

Animals that talk

Spaghetti Drawing

The spaghetti drawing method is a **FOOLPROOF** (nothing personal) way of **creating great** Krappy Kartoons. It's a bit like a drawing version of a **Multiple Choice Test** in that you choose your drawing from a number of different possibilities.

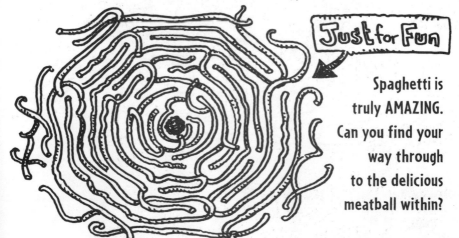

Just for Fun

Spaghetti is truly AMAZING. Can you find your way through to the delicious meatball within?

Here's how it works. Instead of trying to nut out where all those pesky lines are meant to go **EXACTLY**, just start drawing. For every line you think you'll need, draw about ten extra. You'll end up with a picture that looks a lot like **a big serve of spaghetti!** Yum!

OK, all the right lines should be there.
It's just a matter of getting old **Mr Rubber** out
and taking away all the lines you don't need.
Simple.

It's Surfin' Bob

Hey, but I... CAN'T SURF!

You can then redraw or trace over your picture...

Whoops... Spaghetti drawing is also handy for showing **CHAOS** and **MAYHEM** - vital tools for the Krappy Kartoonist.

Oh dear.
Can you find poor old Surfin' Bob now?

Have you heard of the **RENAISSANCE?** It was probably the greatest Art Movement in history! And where did it happen? Italy!!! And where does **SPAGHETTI** come from? That's right, **ITALY!!!** Proof (if any more was needed) of the creative **POWER** of **SPAGHETTI!**

ITALY 1497

Leonardo da Vinci, inspired by his mum's cooking, paints 'The Last Supper'.

Hey Leo, no dessert until you finish your supper!

Aww...Mum!

At the same time in IRELAND

With only boiled potato soup to inspire him, all that poor old Declan Kelly (my ancestor) could hope to achieve was a very crude version of 'Mr Potato Head'.

Declan, stop playing with your food!

Aww, Mum!

THE INSIDE SCOOP ON DRAWING KARTOON BODIES

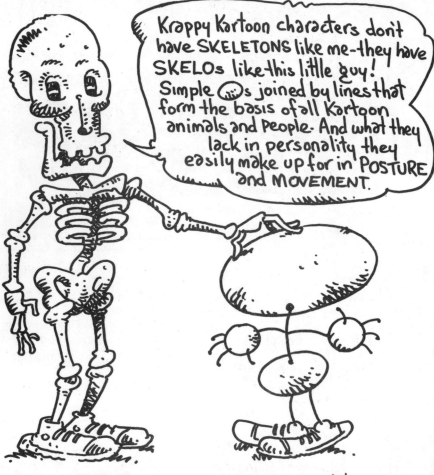

Krappy Kartoon characters don't have SKELETONS like me - they have SKELOs like this little guy! Simple ⊙s joined by lines that form the basis of all kartoon animals and people. And what they lack in personality they easily make up for in POSTURE and MOVEMENT.

And that's how we use them – they are a quick way of working out how to draw a character's body in different poses.

20

OK, the first thing to do is to get down to basics. Let's use our **'KK X-Ray Specs'** to have a look at the Skelos beneath these two Kartoons.

Good… nice and **simple,** just how we Krappy Kartoonists **like it!** Now all that's needed is to move these lines and shapes around to create different poses.

Who turned out the lights?

Sniff Sniff

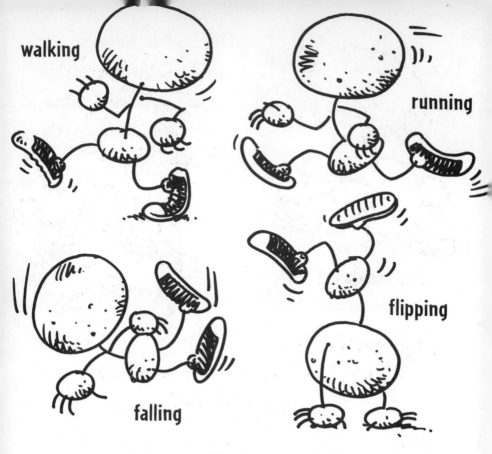

walking

running

flipping

falling

With no clothes, hair or fur to get in the way it's easy to see how the pose works, and because Skelos are so quick to draw you can keep trying different versions until it's right.

begging

playing dead

jumping

When you have the right pose, use it as a base for your character. Draw in the outer body shape and then continue adding details.

You can do this by either tracing over your Skelo or just using it as a guide for a new drawing.

By quickly sketching out different combinations, you can also use **Skelos** as a **fast way** to find out the ideal body shape for a character.

Which body do you think is best for **Mr Fishbreath** here? The KK's new trainee assistant to the backup deputy vice-principal.

Giant extinct Kartoons known only from their fossilised **SKELOs** have been found throughout the world. Experts think that these ancient **MEGA KARTOONS** – distant relatives of many of today's popular characters – were rubbed out 65 million years ago when a huge **RUBBER METEOR** hit the earth.

MICASAURUS

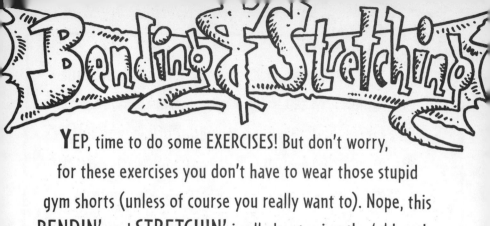

Bending & Stretching

YEP, time to do some EXERCISES! But don't worry, for these exercises you don't have to wear those stupid gym shorts (unless of course you really want to). Nope, this BENDIN' and STRETCHIN' is all about using the 'old nut' – your noodle…you know, that thing that rattles when you run!?! Your **BRAIN,** dummy. What??? You forgot it!!! OH WELL, that's OK, it's mostly optional for KK stuff anyway!

Now, KARTOONS are drawings that have been stretched and bent out of shape. Which technically means they're

EXAGGERATIONS!!!

warning!

OK, this word is FAR too long for this book, especially given the brain shortage situation. Let's just stick to **BEND** and **STRETCH**.

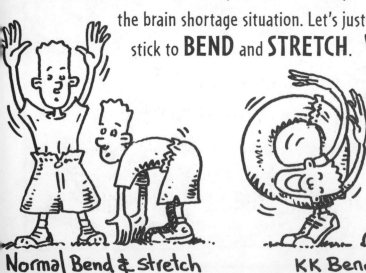

Normal Bend & Stretch

KK Bend & Stretch

Now how do we learn to bend and stretch our drawings? Well, let's use a shape that's already bent and try stretching our kartoon to fit into it. And what better **BENT SHAPE** to use than that of the most Noble of the Yellow Fruits...

"THE BANANA"

So get you a banana.

Let's trace our banana.

Great, now we can eat our banana. **YUM!** With this cool shape we are now going to make a **KARTOON CHARACTER!** But hang on, maybe one's **TOO EASY!** Let's make a whole family of characters: **THE BENDER FAMILY.**

First up will be **GRANDPA BENDER**. Now the simple secret is (and promise you won't tell anyone) that if you put eyes, a nose and a mouth onto any shape, you're well over halfway to making a face. And if it's a funny shape, then there's a good chance it'll be a **FUNNY FACE**. Let's see…

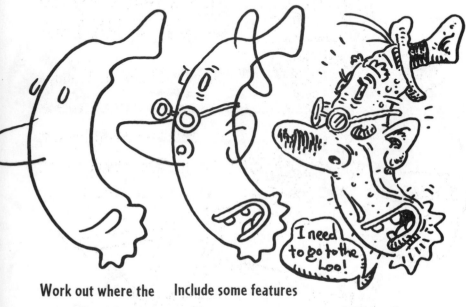

Work out where the eyes, nose and mouth will go.

Include some features that are common to grandpas.

Add details.

Most grandpas like funny hats, wear glasses and often forget to shave.

"Ta Da!"

Here's Grandpa Bender, and notice how the **bendy banana shape** works just as well for his **BODY** as...

Oh dear, I think old Grandpa Bender has had a little accident! Why don't we go visit the rest of the family while he...er, sorts this out.

I told you I had to go!!!

29

The Bender Family

Mother Bender

Lil' Sis Bender

Rude Brother Bender

30

Scratch the Dog

Seedie the Budgie

Fergus the Ferret???

OK, that's the Benders. And wow, look at the
FAMILY RESEMBLANCE that comes from using the
same **FUNNY SHAPE!** Bit like families that all have
big bums – or sticky-out ears. This family is just **BENT!**

So now you know how to exercise the KK way, grab a shape –
ANY SHAPE – and start your **Bendin' & Stretchin'!**

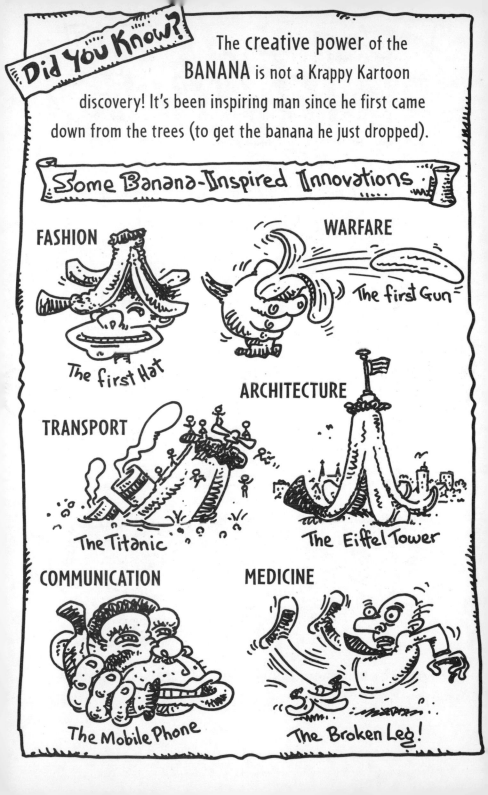

Shadows

…are a surefire way of bringing your Krappy Kartoons to life and making them **jump off the page!** Let's get Bob here to give us a **DEMO**. OK, Bob, let's see if you can jump without a shadow.

Nope, pretty disappointing! Now let's try it **with** a SHADOW.

Yep, much better, but I think Bob could **try** a bit harder – don't you?

So, the **greater** the **distance** between
Bob and the **shadow**, the **higher** Bob appears.

When there is no space between Bob
and the shadow, it shows he is standing on the ground.
A shadow behind him indicates he's next to a wall.

How to Draw Krappy Shadows

Shadows are simple **FLATTENED** versions of the things that cast them. Take this little bunny, for instance.

Let's flatten him out so we can get an idea of what his **shadow** will look like.

Nice.
Now it's just a matter of filling in the shape and getting another stand-in bunny for **BUNNY SHADOW PERFECTION.**

The Sun

Light

Knowing where the **light** is coming from is the most **important** part of drawing shadows. The sun is a good bet. Now using a simple shape like a circle, imagine it as a **3D** ball. The light would hit the nearest side leaving the far side dark.

Shadows form on the far side of the object from the light.

Each shape you then add to your picture should also have the **same** light and dark side.

The nose sticks out so it also casts a new shadow on the shape.

So, when drawing just imagine you're wearing those krappy 3D glasses (and hey, we know how well they work)!

I'm just a shadow of my former shape

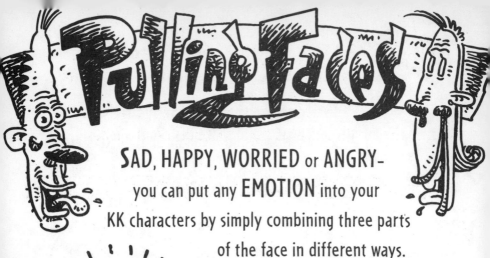

Pulling Faces

SAD, HAPPY, WORRIED or ANGRY—
you can put any EMOTION into your
KK characters by simply combining three parts
of the face in different ways.

① THE EYEBALL

② THE MOUTH

 ③ THE EYEBROW

The NOSE is only there
for COMIC RELIEF,
so we'll just ignore
it for now.

Did you hear what happened when the Nose went out with the Tissue? He blew it!

OK , we'll keep it simple for starters and a **SMILEY FACE** is about as **SIMPLE** as it gets! Look at the **EMOTIONS** you can make just by combining the mouth and eyes using three different shapes.

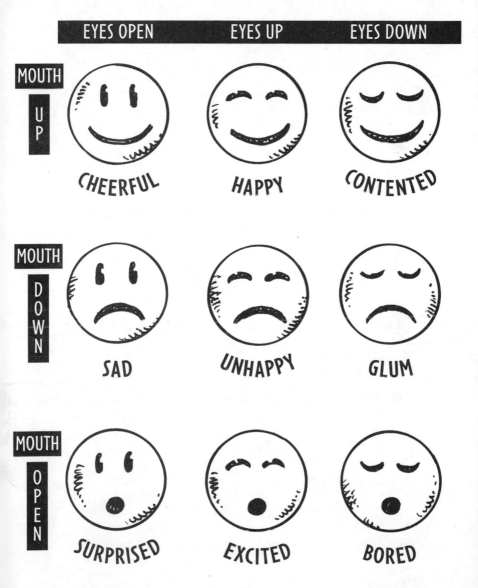

	EYES OPEN	EYES UP	EYES DOWN
MOUTH UP	CHEERFUL	HAPPY	CONTENTED
MOUTH DOWN	SAD	UNHAPPY	GLUM
MOUTH OPEN	SURPRISED	EXCITED	BORED

If we now start to include **EYEBROWS,** many more complex emotions are possible.

HURT   EVIL   WORRIED

STRAINING   SHOCKED   SMUG

Remember, these are cartoons so you can also add little **speech bubbles.** They help to highlight the emotion and at the same time add a bit more humour!

RELIEVED   ANNOYED   CLUMSY

NERVOUS   DEVIOUS   ANGRY

The next step is to add white around the eyes.
This allows you to make the eyes look in a certain direction,
which can help show what a character is **thinking**.

Hey, and the **mouth** is starting to do **its own thing**…
why don't we take a closer look?

Let's see how **the mouth** can do emotions all on **its own.**

But first we'll need to limber up with some exercises!

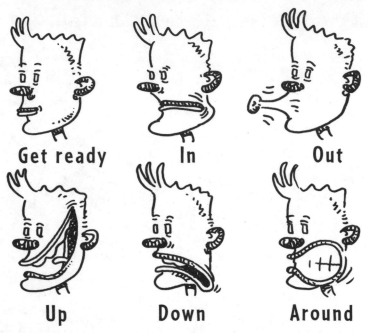

Get ready   In   Out

Up   Down   Around

TIP

When drawing an emotion, go into the bathroom and make the face you want to draw in the mirror. This will not only help you work out the expression you need, but will at the same time SERIOUSLY confuse the rest of your family!

Good, now let's make **some faces!**

Scared

Crazy

Glum

Rude

Cold

Full

Scary...

more **SCARY...**

(**gulp**, maybe too scary)

Now we know how to do simple expressions,
let's concentrate on just one and explore how to draw the
different **VARIATIONS** of that **EXPRESSION**.

This is Mary. She's going to show us how to look <u>CROSS</u>!

Hi

Now, Mary, get cross.

OK! Crosser!!!

Get ANGRY, Mary

Come on, Mo-o-o-re! Go <u>BERKO</u>!!

...!?!

Oops…!!! Maybe CROSS wasn't the best expression to start with – let's try something a little **nicer**.

This is Mary's twin sister Anne. She's going to do HAPPY!

Give us a smile, Anne.

Come on… a BIG SMILE.

More, HAPPIER, WIDER!

"STR-E-ETCH" BE HAPPY …..!?!

Well, mmm…we don't seem to have any more volunteers but I hope you get the idea.

How to achieve **WORLD PEACE** the Krappy Kartoon way!

~ BAN EYEBROWS ~

That's right!

If everyone in the world SHAVED OFF their **EYEBROWS**, cross, **angry** people would be a thing of the past.

Even a slight frown would be impossible.

Peace would break out **everywhere**.

Just take a look at this evil Dictator bent on death and destruction!

Shave off his eyebrows and he just looks confused. No one will be taking him seriously now!

The KK **peace movement** begins at home!

Next time your dad falls asleep on the couch, get his razor, sneak in and shave off his eyebrows! Believe me, you'll notice **a sharp change** in **attitude** when he wakes up.

46

EARS

Ears aren't just for holding up hats!

They're a vital tool for the Krappy Kartoonist.

Long overlooked in favour of the more high-profile NOSE

and MOUTH, ears have only recently begun to really

stick out – where they belong!!!

Ears are just NATURALLY FUNNY.

Take a look!

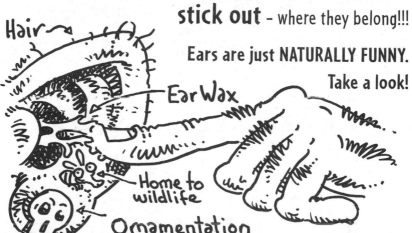

Hair

Ear Wax

Home to wildlife

Ornamentation

The first Law of FUNNY EARS was discovered by the great ALBERT EARSTINE

They should always stick out at a 90° angle from the head – EARS EQUAL MANS CRANIUM SQUARED

$E = MC^2$

90°

You can **stick things** in your ears to make your
Krappy Kartoons even **funnier!!!**

EXAMPLES

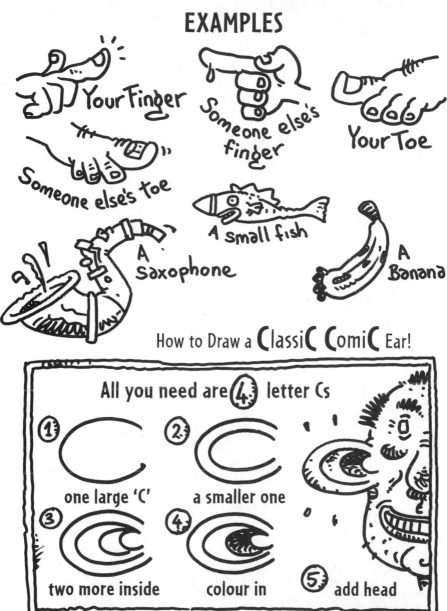

Your Finger

Someone else's finger

Your Toe

Someone else's toe

A small fish

A Saxophone

A Banana

How to Draw a **Classic Comic** Ear!

All you need are ④ letter Cs

① one large 'C'

② a smaller one

③ two more inside

④ colour in

⑤ add head

Vincent Van Gogh was a Famous Artist but the man never painted a funny picture in his life! He knew how silly ears are and was so worried that his self-portrait (with ear) would not be taken seriously, **HE CUT IT OFF!!!** No joke!

This was hailed by the **ART WORLD** as an act of **TRUE GENIUS** and a mighty blow against Krappy Drawing everywhere. But sadly, he didn't live long enough to enjoy his new-found fame. Soon afterwards he was **run over** by a bus when his hat slipped down over his eyes as he was crossing the street.

Ear today gone tomorrow

It's an end to an Artistic Eara!

Ear's all that's left of poor old Vincent

1. THE NOSE

Have you ever thought just how **REALLY ODD** noses are? Hollow lumps of flesh, sticking out of the middle of a face! Hairy on the inside, knobbly on the outside – with a more than occasional habit of **LEAKING**! Yep, the nose is a **CRAZY** thing, so making FUN of it is pretty simple. Basically you can't **BLOW IT!**

A **good trick** to remember with noses is **not** to draw them straight on. It tends to hide the shape and also how far it **sticks out** (the very things that make the nose funny).

Nose straight on is flat and boring

Bend slightly to the side and the true nose appears

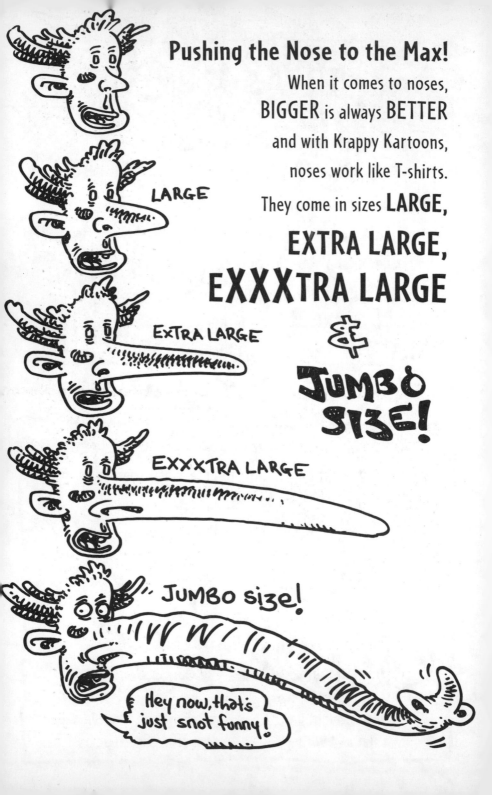

Drawing UGLY

In Krappy Kartoon Land, we LOVE the **UGLY!**
It's just so much more INTERESTING and FUN to draw than
'the nice' or 'the pretty' or 'the BEAUTIFUL!' Plus being a
Krappy Drawer means your stuff is **naturally** UGLY
anyway – and hey, it's always best to go with your strengths.

Which would you rather Draw?

A Lovely Red Glowing Sunset

A Lonely Red-Bottomed Baboon

If you said the BABOON, then you are right,
a winner and definitely a Krap Drawer. Read on…
If you said the sunset, then **yikes**…are you ever
reading the wrong book!!

Unfortunately, not everything in the world is UGLY. Sometimes we need to **modify** people and objects so that they conform to the KK New World Order.

Gorgeous George gets the Krappy Kartoon
Total Make-Over

George is a guy who enjoys workouts at the gym, long walks on the beach and is an expert on the history of Hair Gel. BO-O-O-O-RING!!!

Perfect, just Perfect!

First we need to do something about that pert little nose.

Now bring the chin back and add a couple more.

Add one big bulging eyeball.

Transplant hair curl to chin.
Shave head.

Knock out some teeth and
thicken ears.

Add various spots, pimples,
drool, etc. **All done!**

Grotty George
is a bloke who likes
burping in movie
theatres, scratching
his bum and collecting
used tissues.

Me feel
like new
man, thanks
to Krappy
Kartoons!

Ugly and disgusting things you can add to your Kartoons.

A smelly doggy poo...

dead rat...

pus-spitting,
brain-sucking Alien...

insides of your school
bag by term 3...

your maths teacher...

or a plate of
steaming vegetables
(Mmm... maybe that's
going a bit too far!)

Things can become **UNEXPECTEDLY UGLY** with just a little Krappy Kartoon Know-how!

Is this a **fluffy white bunny** in a field of **red poppies?**

No, step back, **'go the UGLY'** and it becomes
Hunting Season with a real **BUNNY BLAST!**

There's 'cute' and then there's KRAPPY KARTOON KUTE!

OK, we've done UGLY, so now let's do CUTE. **'Wha-a-a-at?'** I hear you say. 'After all that stuff in the last chapter about beautiful being **BO-O-O-ORING!?!** What gives?' Well, it's like this. Cute isn't actually beautiful and it isn't ugly either. It's this weird **'third state of being'** and it definitely has a place in the KK world of the wacky.

Take a baby, for instance. Everyone knows that babies are **CUTE**, but what does that mean? **BABIES** are certainly not **BEAUTIFUL!**

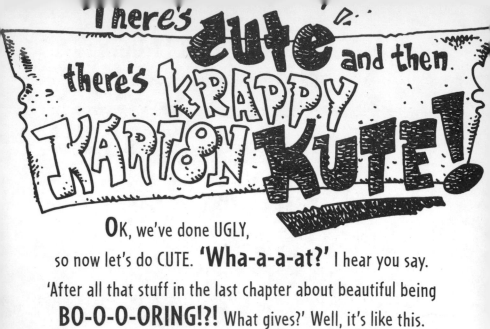

Toxic Smell →

← No Hair

Huge Bug-like Eyes →

Ears stick out

Piggy Nose →

Fat little bodie with no discernible muscle definition

Drool →

Yep, all the telltale signs of the UGLY…and yet babies are still **strangely appealing.** How does that work? Well, the answer is MOTHER NATURE and her Five **Laws of Cute.**

She knows that babies need an edge…a trick to get parents to even go near them. Let's face it, who in their right mind would??? Crying, pooing, weeing, smelly lumps who can't even wipe their own bottoms! So she invented these **five laws** to make the little horrors a little bit more user-friendly and just plain irresistible.

THE 5 LAWS of CUTE

1. Large head and small body
2. Big wide glassy eyes
3. Little upturned nose
4. Big feet, small hands
5. Small mouth and tiny ears

With this information we Krappy Kartoonists are now FREE to take and subvert these LAWS for our own twisted Krappy Kartoon ends!

Ruff

Let's see what happens when we apply the **Five Laws of Cute** to this very ordinary cartoon dog!

Little ears →

Big head →

Small Body →

→ Big shiny eyes

← Small nose and mouth

Large feet

Mmm…definitely CUTER but not KK KUTE.
We need to push **'The Cute'** to the max!

Oh boy – now that's what I call a **KUTE DOG!**
Cool. So now we know how to draw Kute,
let's have a party to celebrate!

Whoah! That's way too much Kute! Easy stomach!!!
Let this be a lesson. Now you have the power of **KUTE**,
use it wisely. Don't overdo it!

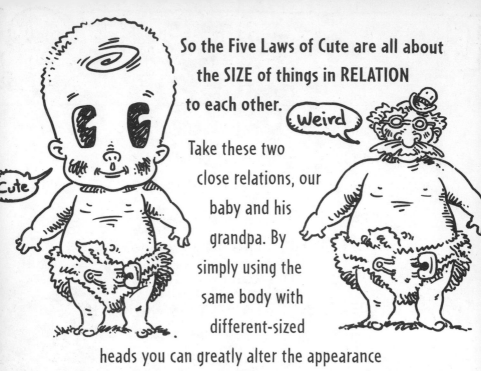

So the Five Laws of Cute are all about the SIZE of things in RELATION to each other.

Take these two close relations, our baby and his grandpa. By simply using the same body with different-sized heads you can greatly alter the appearance and create not only **cute**, but also... **weird**, **gross** and the **downright UGLY!**

(which we love)

How to Draw Big Shiny Eyes

This is probably the **most important** of the Five Laws of Drawing Cute and it's easy to do when you know how! Grab the nearest person – ignore their Bad Breath and look into their eyes. Because EYES are So SMOOTH you'll see a white reflection from the nearest light or window. To get our eyes shiny we need to add in this white dot.

Step 1.

Draw a simple eye outline with a circle inside

Step 2.

Put a square or circle onto one side

Step 3.

Colour in the eye and rub out the line

Tip

In kartoons, eyes don't have to be inside the head. Sometimes it's more fun to draw them on the outside for an Eye-popping effect.

WOW...

Did you Know?

Every RULE has an EXCEPTION. There's one animal which is cuter than any other and yet **NONE** of the Five Laws of Cute apply!

The Baby Elephant

Big Ears
Tiny Eyes
Large Nose
Large Body
Little Feet

Look what happens when we use the Cute rules. **WhoooH!** Now that's just **wrong!**

Making Fun of!

In this chapter you'll learn how to make **FUN** of friends, family, **TEACHERS** - even strangers! Yep, this is the chapter where you'll find out how to do hilarious **CARICATURES!!!**

And hey, it's going to be SO EASY because, let's face it, people are pretty **funny**-looking to begin with. If aliens were to fly down to earth tomorrow, chances are they'd be too busy laughing to bother about all that WORLD DOMINATION stuff! **YES,** man's best hope is not his LARGE BRAIN, but the SILLY HAIRCUT on top of it!

Alien Invasion Defeated by a SWAT team of Elvis Impersonators

So, people are all funny-looking, right? But they also all look very different from each other. In Krappy Kartoon Land we're always ready to CELEBRATE that DIFFERENCE! (**Celebrate** = making fun of **/ Difference** = odd bits) And when you make fun of a person's 'odd bits' in a drawing, it's called a **caricature.**

TiP But before we go off and start making fun of other people, I think it's always best to make fun of yourself. SO …

How to draw GEOFF KELLY

To do a Kartoon of a person, you first have to pick out two or three things that make that person different or ODD! With me it's the shape of my head (blocky), my protruding mouth, and my upturned nose.

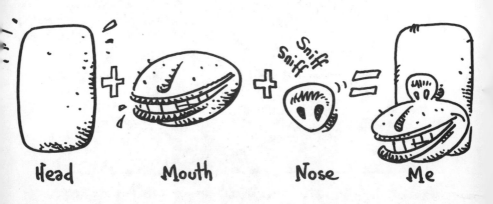

Head   Mouth   Nose   Me

Once you have found those features and combined them, you can then **STRETCH** one or more to make the face even **FUNNIER.**

Then it's just a matter of adding as much detail as you like!

'HA!' I hear you say, 'that's fine when you're Kartoonising someone with a weird head like you! What about normal-looking people? What then?' Well, in KK Land there is **NO NORMAL!** Everyone, and I mean **EVERYONE**, is **ODD!!** Look a little harder and you will soon see just how weird the world really is, or can be with a little KK help.

Take Miss Prim

She's a young teacher who is patient, caring and well-liked by the children in her class. Mmm . . . nothing for the Krappy Kartoonist here . . . or is there? Let's take a closer look!

Long oval-shaped Head

Pointy Nose

Daggy Hairstyle

Wide Mouth

Small Mole (must be exploited)

Small bulge (should not go unnoticed)

Skinny legs

Sensible flat shoes

Yep! Stacks of stuff to work with.

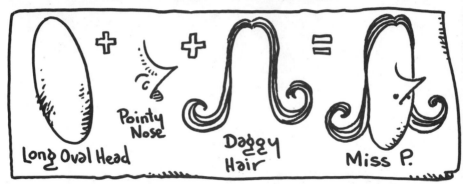

Long Oval Head + Pointy Nose + Daggy Hair = Miss P.

Say Hello to... **Miss Primate**

Throw in some hair on the mole, crazy eyeballs and a wicked smile and then . . .

make up a lame joke to finish off the pic.

What Miss Primate For Lunch

Kartoonising **animals** works much the same way. Let's try using a Koala. Now what features make a Koala a Koala?

Square head   Big Black Nose   Fluffy Ears

Add detail and HEY PRESTO, we have our **Krappy Koala!**

Now let's play around with **changing** the **size** of those three Koala features.

Wow, doesn't matter how you **stretch** them – together they always make a Koala.
AMAZING, HEY?

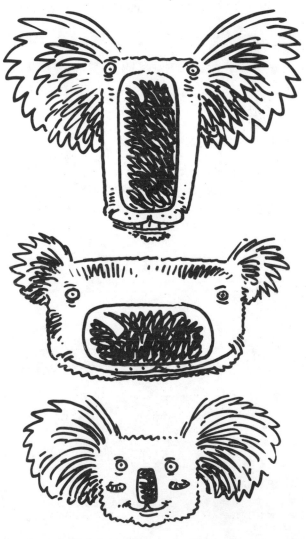

Did You Know?

Just like **snowflakes** or zebras, no two teachers are exactly **alike**. But when it comes to personality (that's right, teachers do have them) they nearly all fall into a small number of groups or types. Which is handy for us Krappy Kartoonists because we can then **EXPLOIT** these **TYPES** for **MAXIMUM HILARITY!** We do this by using characters or things that **represent** those types of personality - for instance... Mr Krud

Mr Krud is one of those strict, gloomy teachers

Darth Vader was pretty gloomy and also quite strict on occasions!

You cannot escape your destiny - MATHS TEST

Save me Luke

I've got a Bad feeling about this!

Combine the two and we get... **Mr Krud as Darf Vader**

Here are some examples of other **TEACHER PERSONALITIES** and possible ways you could draw them. Can you think of any others?

Sporty Teacher

Busy Teacher

Cuddly Teacher

Funny Teacher

COLOUR

Mmm…this could be a pretty short chapter, because as you have probably noticed the **PUBLISHERS** of this book are too **CHEAP** to pay for any colour! But as it's a mighty important part of Good Krappy Drawing, let's see what we can do.

Colour Rule #1

EVERY COLOUR GOES WITH **EVERY OTHER COLOUR**

That's right – there are **NO** bad colour combinations! I know you hear people say, 'This colour doesn't go with that colour' or 'You can't wear those coloured shoes with that coloured dress, Uncle Phil'!

Well, it's **ALL BULL!!!**

Colours are like a Big Family. And as in all families, some get along while others are always **clashing**. It's natural and makes life interesting – and **INTERESTING** is what we want our Krappy Kartoons to be.

74

Don't believe me!?!
Let's try a **LITTLE EXPERIMENT** and see.

We'll colour in a picture using **any old colours** next to each other. Use the number guide on the **RANDOM COLOUR CHART** below to colour in the picture on the next page.

KK Random Colour Chart

1 — colour of your undies

2 — colour of your mum's undies

3 — colour of your granny's undies

4 — colour of your best friend's undies

5 — colour of your teacher's undies

Look, this is getting out of control...

for numbers 6, 7 and 8 just

do a lucky dip in your

undies drawer. OK?

Note: for this experiment to work, all underwear must be no more than three days old.

OK, this should be a **BEAUTIFULLY COLOURED Work of Art** where all the undie colours combine in an interesting and unexpected fashion. Possibly... maybe a bit weird but let's hope in a **good way**! So, the lesson is when it comes to putting colours together (just like picking undies), go with what **feels comfortable** and always **take chances**.

THERE ARE NO RULES

In the wonderful world of Krappy Kartoons, the sky can be GREEN, the ocean YELLOW and the cows BLUE. It's a **made-up** world, a place of pretend – so why be tied down by reality? **Have fun.** Surprise people. I for one would like to see everyone with GREEN EARS and YELLOW LIPS!

The world's most famous painting, the MONA LISA, is really pretty **boring** colour-wise. It's basically **BROWN!** Light brown skin, dark brown hair, brown dress, brown sky and brown land. It's even in a BROWN FRAME. It is DEFINITELY **no** Krappy Picture! Plus she looks far too HAPPY to be a MOANING LISA. Let's give her face the KK treatment and use our undies number chart to jazz up her colour.

MOANING LISA

SOUND EFFECTS

Used the right way, sound effects can be a **FUN** way to add **humour** and **movement** to an otherwise dull, lifeless Krappy Kartoon.

Take a look at this pic. Nothing much happening here!

But add a simple **SOUND EFFECT**...

PHHHHFFFUPH

and it's a **whole new story!**

How to Make a Sound Effect

It's easy! Most words that are used to describe a sound or an action tend to resemble **that** sound or action. Like…

So, you can use these words as they are, or you can make more of the sound by **STRETCHING** the word, just as we stretch our Kartoons. Like…

It looks **funnier** and gives the viewer a better feel for the action/sound involved.

More fun still is to make up your own 'Sound Effect' words. To work out how we do that, let's first ask a question. How does a duck **QUACK**? The answer is - it doesn't!!!

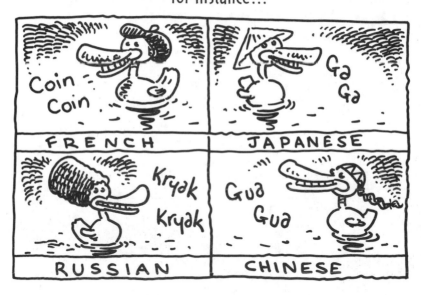

Ducks all over the world make the same noise, right? In English we say 'QUACK' but it's really nothing like the real **DUCK SOUND**!

Other languages all have their own versions, for instance…

FRENCH — Coin Coin

JAPANESE — Ga Ga

RUSSIAN — Kryak Kryak

CHINESE — Gua Gua

There's **no DUCKING** the lesson here. All these **DUCK SOUNDS** work because they don't attempt to spell or pronounce the duck talk which, without a bill, would just be too hard. Instead they simplify the sound, making it a kind of **Kartoon version.** And don't we just love that!

So this means to make up your new SOUND EFFECT you must learn to make FUN of the sound. With this in mind and the happy thought that good spelling is now only optional, let's explore a simple, everyday sound like a...

Now, although I love the idea of kids all over Australia suddenly burping into their books- maybe it's best that you just use your imagination for this exercise!

OK, how to do a BURP? Well, I think we should break it into the three main types.

No.1 THE QUICKIE

This burp sneaks up and happens before you know it. Related to a hiccup, it's like a small explosion that starts big and ends abruptly!

Uurrreph!

No. 2 THE STUTTER

Fast high-pitched stop/start burp that slowly dies out. Sometimes has a surprise lift at the end with a final POP of GAS!

BhPhuu-ue-ue-ueerh!

No. 3 THE WET GARGLE

This one has been building for a long time. Starts small but just keeps getting bigger. Usually involves some fluid escaping.

Use **large letters** for **loud sounds**, small letters for soft sounds. Make your sound effect point to where the noise is coming from and shape the word like a sound wave. Practise on some burps, a hiccup or a few yawns and when you feel up to it have a go at these **more challenging sounds!**

Teeth Brushing

Nose Picking

Finger Scraping

avoiding STUFF

If you want to be a successful Krappy Artist, you need to choose your battles. There's a lot of **REALLY HARD STUFF** to draw out there, and sometimes the best thing to do is simply **RUN AWAY!**

A good Krappy Artist knows when he's **beat!**

The **things** that are hardest to draw differ from artist to artist. Some of **my** least favourites would be…

People playing trombones • Unicorns
Ant-eaters • The Queen of England
Lobsters • Hands

(sends shivers up my pen just writing them down)

Now, most of the time I just choose **NOT** to draw **Hard Stuff** like that. But occasionally, as a professional KK Artist I'm given a tough job that I just can't avoid! Maybe a cover of a new book…

…and the book's called WHEN THE UNICORN PLAYED TROMBONE TO THE QUEEN AS SHE SAT ON AN ANT-EATER EATING A LOBSTER. Can you do it? We need it tomorrow!

Gulp!

The Publisher

The Illustrator

What to do???

I really need the money! Well, when this happens I usually resort to 'the imagination', but not MY imagination… **YOUR IMAGINATION!**

Like so…

WOW!!!

Works a treat and the drawing is so lifelike (although I don't think the Queen really has a moustache!). **What's that?! THE BUSH?** Oh yeah, it kinda, sorta, got in the way! But that's OK. Everything's there – you just have to use your **imagination**. Kids are good at that, **right?**

SO, you get the idea. When it comes to drawing **Hard Stuff** that you **Can't Avoid,** the rule is 'LESS IS MORE' – meaning the **LESS** you draw, the **MORE** the person looking at the picture has to invent.

Using a shadow

Scary things like monsters are really hard to draw, so try just using the **monster's shadow**. It's less work for you, and the viewer will imagine the **scariest** monster they can think of in much more detail than you could ever draw.

Filling in the lines

A Polar Bear is pretty hard to draw too, especially in a snow-storm. You can get the viewers to do MOST of the drawing by putting in just a SMALL amount of detail. They know what a Polar Bear looks like and will mentally fill in the blanks.

Assuming stuff

We all know that businessmen have feet and usually wear shoes (which are pretty hard to draw). Why go to all the trouble of drawing them when we can have our man standing in a puddle (a box or hole would also work)?

HANDS

Hands are a special case. They are so hard to draw! All those nails, fingers, knuckles and such, how are we ever going to HANDLE HANDS? OK, I have just one word for you... **POCKETS!!!** Yep, the Krappy Kartoonist's best friend is the pocket!

Look Mum, no HANDS!

Problem solved

'But', I hear you say, 'you can't have everyone in every picture with their HANDS in their POCKETS!!!' Mmm... well, you could, and it would be kinda funny, but I know where you're coming from. You need some more AVOIDING HANDS VARIETY.

More Non-Handy Hints Try adding these to your pictures.

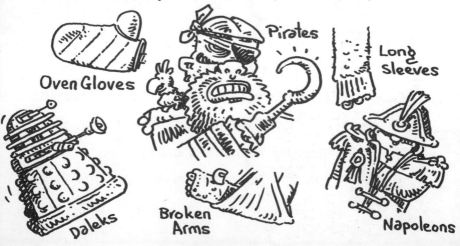

Oven Gloves

Pirates

Long Sleeves

Daleks

Broken Arms

Napoleons

WHAT'S THAT?!? You still want to learn how to **DRAW HANDS?** Even after all I've said about avoiding hard stuff and the miracle of the pocket!!! Well, all I can say to that 'TRY-HARD' sort of an attitude is… **LO-O-O-SER!!!** That's right. LOSER, because all you really need to know about drawing hands is - **THE LOSER SIGN!**

Spot the Difference

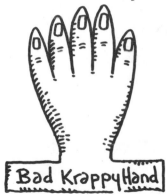

Bad Krappy Hand

Good Krappy Hand

The difference is the **OPPOSABLE THUMB.** Sounds complicated, but as it was invented by a monkey I think you should be able to work it out. Put simply, it means that the thumb sticks out from the side of the hand, making an 'L' shape.

It's the 'L' shape formed by the thumb that makes a hand look like a hand and not a bunch of sausages (see 'Bad Krappy Hand'). So if you remember to always draw the thumb down from the fingers, your 'Bad Krappy Hand Days' are over!

Maths have never been a Krappy Kartoonist's strong point. Sometimes, though, that can work in our favour. Four fingers work fine for a Kartoon Hand, which means one less thing that can go wrong.

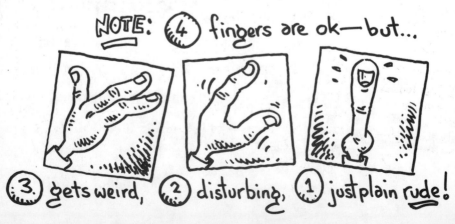

IF ALL ELSE FAILS, TRY ABSTRACT ART

Early last century, some very clever Krappy Artists had the inspired idea of making **PAINTINGS** of **NOTHING!** They figured, 'We can't fail if nobody knows what the paintings are meant to be in the first place'. They called it **ABSTRACT ART**, and to their amazement and delight, people actually started to buy their pictures. They became famous and their work was hung in galleries all around the world! They couldn't believe their luck. What had started as a kind of JOKE meant they could now live the ARTISTIC LIFESTYLE without ever having to learn to **DRAW!!!**

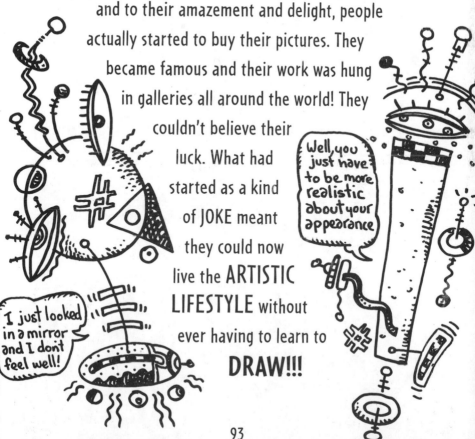

Well, you just have to be more realistic about your appearance

I just looked in a mirror and I don't feel well!

Now you can try **ABSTRACT ART** too.
Although I've never been a big fan of it myself,
the fact that there aren't many (if any) Abstract Artists
of your age means you're sure to be noticed.

The only trouble is that Abstract Art is not quite as easy as it looks! Apart from the basic questions of **where** to start, **when** to stop and **which** way is up, the real trick is to work out how to make something out of nothing – or is it NOTHING out of SOMETHING?

So here are a **few ideas** you could try to get yourself **started.**

1 As a kid, you've been getting into trouble for causing a **MESS** since before you could crawl. It's a NATURAL TALENT that you can use in your Abstract Art. While painting, just pretend you're eating dinner or better still, making a cake!

2 Get those **FAMILY PETS** involved.

3

Try working
BLINDFOLDED.

4 Work from
a **DISTANCE!**

Paint-bombs and water pistols could be **FUN!**

Get a mate over and have an **ARTISTIC ARGUMENT!!!**

OK, it's the end of the **BOOK** so you should be a brilliant **Krappy Kartoonist!** CONGRATULATIONS!

Here's your trophy.

Your name goes here

Er... what's that?

YOU'RE NOT?!? You still can't draw really well?!?

Gulp... well, it's too late to give you your money back!!!

Mmm... maybe there's one more thing ...

I wasn't going to mention it, as it's really **not** in the
Quick Fix spirit of this book. But what the hey, it can't hurt
now! In one word, it's **PRACTICE!** Yeah, yeah, I know...
but don't worry, this is practice the KK way.

Yes, now let's talk about DOODLES.

Hey, stop **snickering** and wipe that **grin** off your face.

I'm not talking about THAT sort of DOODLE! This is a chapter

about **Drawing a Doodle!!!** No, now that didn't come out

right! Let's see…this is a chapter where we'll learn to draw

USING a **DOODLE!!!** No, that's not right either.

Look, stop **GIGGLING!** OK, that's it, I'm going to have

to start this chapter again…

Look, you know what kids are like. There's no way we'll get through this book using the 'D' word!

Agreed! OK, let's make up a new word for those silly little free-range drawings. Like…

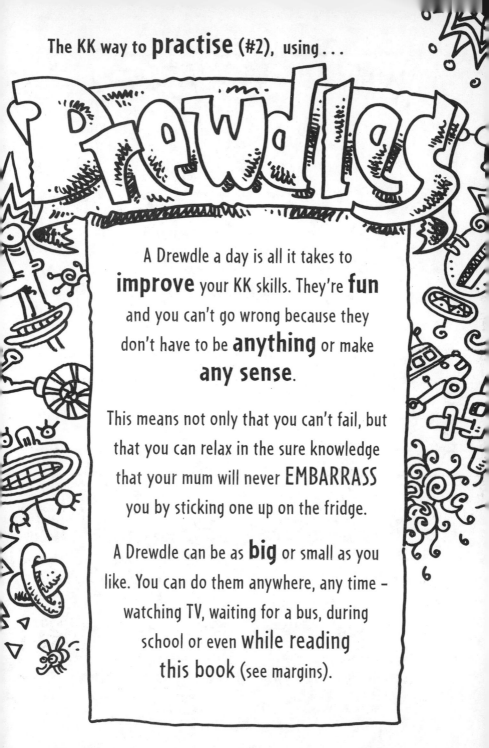

Drewdles!

A Drewdle a day is all it takes to **improve** your KK skills. They're **fun** and you can't go wrong because they don't have to be **anything** or make **any sense**.

This means not only that you can't fail, but that you can relax in the sure knowledge that your mum will never EMBARRASS you by sticking one up on the fridge.

A Drewdle can be as **big** or small as you like. You can do them anywhere, any time – watching TV, waiting for a bus, during school or even **while reading this book** (see margins).

99

The main idea is to just draw.

Don't think and let the pencil take control.

Drewdles are exercises that allow the true Krappy Artist

hidden away in all of us to emerge.

Close your eyes and feel the Krap...be one

with the Krap...**let the KRAP be with you!!!**

Ummmm

Now, there are two main types of Drewdle exercises,
the **pattern** and the **object**.

The Pattern

Start with a simple shape or line and then build around it with lines, dots, swirls or squiggles.

WARNING: Pattern Drewdles have been known to get out of control and swallow up complete notebooks, homework sheets and whole magazines. The author recommends keeping a rubber or white-out handy at all times during these exercises.

The Object

It's similar to the pattern, but you draw **real things**.
Doesn't matter what- the more unexpected the better.
Starting with an eyeball is always a good bet - add
a shape for the head, some features and away you go.

Who knows what
will happen or where
you'll end up?

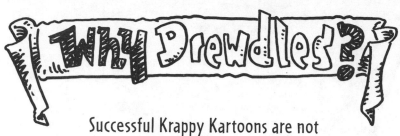

Why Drewdles?

Successful Krappy Kartoons are not
just about **DRAWING TRICKS** but also
about **TAKING CHANCES!** You now know the tricks,
so it's just a matter of learning how to take those chances.
Drewdles are a drawing **SAFETY NET** where you can try
things out without the risk of falling
flat on your...

Ready when you are!

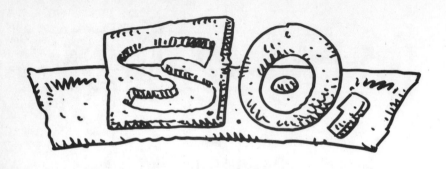

that's Doodles/Drewdles and that's it for the book.

Good luck with the drawing. Remember to have fun!
LOTS OF FUN!!! And consider this – you might always be
a KRAPPY DRAWER, you might always do KRAPPY PICTURES,
but if you **love** drawing and do those pictures REALLY
WELL, you might…one day…just possibly…become
a really RICH and really, really FAMOUS…
**GREAT KRAPPY KARTOON
ARTIST!**